THE HISTORY OF ENGLAND

THE HISTORY OF ENGLAND

FROM THE REIGN OF

HENRY THE 4TH

TO THE DEATH OF

CHARLES THE 1ST

JANE AUSTEN

Introduction by A. S. Byatt

A Note on the Text by Deirdre Le Faye

ALGONQUIN BOOKS OF CHAPEL HILL

1993

Published by
ALGONQUIN BOOKS OF CHAPEL HILL
Post Office Box 2225
Chapel Hill, North Carolina 27515-2225

a division of
Workman Publishing Company, Inc.
708 Broadway
New York, New York 10003

Published in association with
The British Library and The Folio Society.

Library of Congress Cataloging-in-Publication Data

Austen, Jane, 1775-1817.

The history of England : from the reign of Henry the 4th to the death of Charles the 1st / Jane Austen.
p. cm.
ISBN 1-56512-055-8
1. Great Britain—History—Lancaster and York, 1399-1485—Humor.
2. Great Britain—History—Early Stuarts, 1603-1649—Humor.
3. Great Britain—History—Tudors, 1485-1603—Humor. 4. England—Humor.
I. Title.
PR4034.H57 1993
823'.7—dc20 93-17637
CIP
10 9 8 7 6 5 4 3 2 1
First Edition

Introduction

A. S. Byatt

"Girls of fifteen are always laughing," wrote Virginia Woolf in an essay on the young Jane Austen. "But they are crying the moment after. They have no fixed abode from which they see that there is something eternally laughable in human nature." Jane Austen, however, Woolf goes on, was different. "At fifteen she had few illusions about other people and none about herself. Whatever she writes is finished and turned and set in its relation, not to the parsonage but to the universe. She is impersonal, she is inscrutable."

Other writers have often responded with the same sort of absolute enthusiasm to Jane Austen's youthful work. They recognise an unusual mixture of lively energy and gleefully confident control—a true writer, taking charge of her materials, language, and form. G. K. Chesterton, who wrote a preface to an American edition of her early works, called her "elemental," "original," and "exuberant." "She was the very reverse of a starched or a starved spinster; she could have been a buffoon like the Wife of Bath if she chose. This is what gives an infallible force to her irony."

What is interesting to a modern reader in Jane Austen's *History* is its tone. Like all her youthful works it is poking high-spirited fun at conventional writing. *Love and Freindship* poked fun at the contemporary novel of sensibility, with its heroines who "fainted alternately on a sofa," and finally died of too many fainting-fits. "Beware of swoons, dear Laura . . . A frenzy fit is not one quarter so pernicious; it is an exercise to the Body and if not too violent, is I dare say conducive to Health in its consequences—Run mad as often as you chuse; but do not faint."

The *History of England* is poking fun at matter-of-fact abridgements of history, in which deaths and disasters are reduced to educational *facts* to be digested. It is somewhere between deadpan farce in tone, and a kind of wild early irony. That irony appears to me to be directed not at the reader, nor even at the characters, but at the narrator of that work, who is cheerfully presented at the outset as "a partial, prejudiced, & ignorant Historian." Jane Austen's first two published novels were *Pride and Prejudice* and *Sense and Sensibility* and the narrator of the history is a shining example not only of prejudice but of sensibility, as it is mocked in the wildly romantic heroines of *Love and Freindship* and more subtly and with more qualifications in *Sense and Sensibility's* Marianne Dashwood. The "prejudice" of this *History's* narrator is blatant—she means "only to vent my Spleen *against*, & to shew my hatred *to* all those people whose parties or principles do not suit with mine, & not to give information."

Heroines in the novel of sensibility are always wonderfully beautiful and wonderfully sensitive. Jane Austen's prejudiced historian apparently shares the priorities of these novelists, as can be seen in her ranking of the arguments for the innocence of Anne Boleyn.

> It is however but Justice, & my Duty to declare that this amiable Woman was entirely innocent of the Crimes with which she was accused, of which her Beauty, her Elegance, & her Sprightliness were sufficient proofs, not to mention her solemn protestations of Innocence, the weakness of the Charges against her, & the King's

> Character; all of which add some confirmation, tho' perhaps but slight ones when in comparison with those before alledged in her favour.

Scholars have shown that Austen's marginal notes in the family copy of Goldsmith's *History of England* display the same attachment to the cause of the unfortunate Stuarts as this *History*—at one point she wrote, "A family who were always ill used Betrayed or neglected—whose virtues are seldom allowed while their errors are never forgotten," under which some later family member has pencilled, "Bravo Aunt Jane, just my opinion of the case."

I was rather surprised as an adult scholar to discover that Jane Austen *was* on the side of the Stuarts, since I had always supposed, since reading the *History* as a young girl myself, that the narrator was so palpably foolish, prejudiced, romantically silly, and illogical that Jane Austen's true opinions must be the exact opposite of the ones so confidently and absurdly put forward. I was only too ready to think this, since I had grown up with all the opposite prejudices, and saw Mary Queen of Scots as a silly, incompetent, and treacherous woman who plotted incessantly to murder one of the very few intelligent women ever to hold power, and one who moreover wrote exquisite and passionate prose, Elizabeth I of England. Elizabeth, with her shrewdness, her quickness, her *sense*, was my heroine, and from what I knew of Jane Austen from reading her works, I should have supposed that Elizabeth would be her heroine too. And indeed one way of reading the gleeful self-mockery of the *History* is to suppose that "the destroyer of all comfort, the deceitful Betrayer of trust reposed in her, & the Murderess of her Cousin" is the secret Heroine, the representative of Sense and prudence I want her to be.

That this is possible is an indication that the young writer has difficulties with her tone. She genuinely wants sympathy for the slaughtered Queen of Scots and her grandson, Charles I, but can nevertheless continue to poke fun at them. There is something deliciously and uncomfortably comic in her description of the five who were loyal to Charles, and "never forgot the duty of the Subject or swerved from their attachment to his Majesty." These five begin with "The King himself, ever stedfast in his own support"—a sharply ironic note, slipped in amongst the girlish enthusiasm.

In the works of Jane Austen's girlhood all the reader's admiration and sympathy go to the flamboyant skill of that virtuoso narrator, the shifting in and out of madly inadequate stock responses, all exaggerated and delighted in. In *Sense and Sensibility*, I remember, when I read it as a child, younger than the Jane Austen who wrote this *History*, I suffered every inch with Elinor and her attempts to think and feel charitably and justly, and I was consoled by the imperious authority of the witty authorial voice which could say harshly delicious things like, "He was not an ill-disposed young man, unless to be rather cold-hearted, and rather selfish, is to be ill-disposed" (of John Dashwood) and, of Mr. Palmer, "His temper might be a little soured by finding, like many others of his sex, that through some unaccountable bias in favour of beauty, he was the husband of a very silly woman." It was as though the capacity to make these discriminations made up in some way for the powerlessness of Elinor's situation.

The observation about beauty is the ironic opposite of the sentimental predisposition in its favour of the Romantic narrator of the *History*. But the authoritative voice, gleefully judging, is the same.

A Note on the Text

Deirdre Le Faye

"But history, real solemn history, I cannot be interested in . . . I read it a little as a duty, but it tells me nothing that does not either vex or weary me. The quarrels of popes and kings, with wars or pestilences, in every page; the men all so good for nothing, and hardly any women at all—it is very tiresome: and yet I often think it odd that it should be so dull, for a great deal of it must be invention. The speeches that are put into the heroes' mouths, their thoughts and designs—the chief of all this must be invention, and invention is what delights me in other books."—So complains the seventeen-year-old Catherine Morland, in *Northanger Abbey*, to the kindly amusement of Mr. and Miss Tilney.

When Jane Austen was herself barely sixteen, "real solemn history" left her neither puzzled nor plaintive, but instead determined to fight back, with her favorite weapon of ridicule. So it was that during the autumn of 1791 she gleefully composed *her* History of England—sketchy, illogical, and crazily confused, as befitted the work of a "partial, prejudiced, and ignorant Historian"—and after she had copied it neatly into her manuscript book *Volume the Second*, her elder sister Cassandra added coloured illustrations as deliberately misleading as the text, portraying the monarchs not as royal heads of state but as contemporary and sometimes disreputable-looking ordinary people.

The work which Jane parodied was Oliver Goldsmith's four-volume *The History of England from The Earliest Times to the Death of George II* (1771). This publication, offering as it did a comprehensive even though very shallow overview of English history, became an instant success as a schoolroom textbook, to the extent that Goldsmith himself prepared a cheaper and so even more popular one-volume *Abridgement* of the *History* in 1774. A copy of the 1771 four-volume edition which is still preserved in the family archive shows that it was used by the Austen children—small marks and dates at the ends of paragraphs suggest that portions were set aside for daily or weekly study. Volumes III and IV bear numerous interjections and comments in the margins, written by the youthful Jane, registering her disapproval of Goldsmith's Whig view of history and her support for the Stuart family in all its generations. The woodcut circular medallions that head the chapters, containing portraits—more or less imaginary—of the monarchs, have also been gaily coloured in, and show at once that Cassandra parodied the illustrations just as Jane parodied the text.

Jane's *History of England* was neither her first attempt at creative writing nor her first essay into the world of burlesque. According to her own memories, from the age of twelve onwards (1787) she had spent more of her spare time in literary composition than in serious study; while this may have been a matter of mild regret to her in later life, for the modern reader it can only be accounted a blessing. The Austens were a highly intelligent family, and the children received every encouragement from their parents to develop their individual talents; Jane's eldest brother James, indeed, was so advanced in his studies as to matriculate at St. John's College, Oxford, at the age of fourteen. Between 1782 and 1788, under James's guidance, amateur theatrical productions were mounted at Steventon rectory during the Christmas and midsummer holidays, for which he usually wrote versified prologues and epilogues. During his Oxford years he also edited and largely composed a monthly magazine called *The Loiterer*, and family tradition recalled that he had a large share in directing Jane's reading and forming her taste.

With James's example always before her, it is hardly surprising that the young Jane should have been inspired to compose her own stories and short dramatic scenes, to be read aloud for the family's amusement as they sat together in the evenings or to be included in the theatrical programs. She plunged at once into the creation of her own world of black comedy—a world which, although formed within the conventions of the contemporary novel and described in its elegant and high-flown diction, nevertheless contains wildly incredible situations and characters who ruthlessly commit the seven deadly sins with cheerful amorality and great success.

Twenty-six of these items of juvenilia, dating from ca. 1787 to early 1793, were preserved by Jane, and over a period of time in later years she made a "collected edition," copying them into three quarto notebooks, entitled by her *Volume the First*, *Volume the Second*, and *Volume the Third*. These notebooks were not then put away and forgotten, for their well-worn appearance shows that they were continually reread; indeed, as late as in Jane's letter to Cassandra of 23 August 1814 there is a reference to the story *Love and Freindship*, written in 1790; and it seems that Jane was prepared also to show her youthful essays to her brother James's elder children, Anna and James-Edward, once they had reached their teens.

The History of England is uncannily prophetic of Sellar's and Yeatman's *1066 And All That* (1930)—they subtitled their work, "A Memorable History of England, comprising all the parts you can remember including one hundred and three good things, five bad kings, and two genuine dates," and explained further; "History is not what you thought. *It is what you can remember.*" Jane's approach is identical—accepting that for most people the only memories of their history lessons will be a few names and anecdotes of kings and battles, jutting out like rocks from a vast sea of forgetfulness. To increase the confusion of her readers, Jane claimed textual authority from works of fiction, citing Shakespeare's historical plays, Sheridan's comedy *The Critic* (1779), and historical romances such as Charlotte Smith's *Emmeline* (1788) and Sophia Lee's *The Recess* (1785).

She also brought in the names of family and friends—Mrs. Lefroy, Mrs. Knight, and her own brother Francis, then aged seventeen and already away at sea; in the chapter on Elizabeth Tudor, it is he who is mentioned in the same breath as Sir Francis Drake.

After Jane's death in 1817, her sister Cassandra kept many of her letters, other fragmentary manuscripts, and these three notebooks, until her own death in 1845. She then bequeathed *Volume the First* to her youngest brother Charles ("a few of the trifles in this Vol: were written expressly for his amusement—"), *Volume the Third* to her nephew James-Edward, and *Volume the Second* to Francis—no doubt because of this reference to him in *The History of England.*

Volume the Second is bound in vellum, once white but now yellow-brown with age and handling, and splashed and smeared with ink. There are 254 pages as numbered by Jane. On the front cover she inscribed "Volume the Second," large and clear; the title may also have been written on the spine, but if so it is now illegible. At the top of the first page, above the list of "Contents," she wrote "*Ex dono mei Patris*"; in the eighteenth century it was not expected that girls should formally learn Latin, but Jane had evidently picked up enough knowledge of the language from her father and elder brothers to understand and appreciate classical tags and allusions, as can also be seen in her letters in later years.

The notebook descended in Francis's family to one of his granddaughters and then to her niece. It was sold at Sotheby's on 6 July 1977, and purchased by The British Library. The latest and now fully annotated edition of all three *Volumes* is *Catharine and Other Writings* (Margaret Anne Doody and Douglas Murray, OUP, The World's Classics series, 1993). This facsimile edition, however, is the first to have been published. The full spirit of the original work is now made available to all lovers of Jane Austen's writing.

The History of England from the reign of Henry the 4th to the death of Charles the 1st.

By a partial, prejudiced, & ignorant Historian.

To Miss Austen eldest daughter of the Rev: George Austen, this work is inscribed with all due respect by

The Author

N. B. There will be very few Dates in this History.

Henry the 4th

Henry the 4th ascended the throne of England much to his own satisfaction in the year 1399, after having prevailed on his cousin & predecessor Richard the 2d, to resign it to him, & to retire for the rest of his Life to Pomfret Castle, where he happened to be murdered. It is to be supposed that Henry was married, since he had certainly four sons, but it is not in my power to inform the Reader who was his wife. Be this as it may, he did

ot live for ever, but falling ill, his son the Prince
f Wales came and took away the crown; whereupon
he King made a long speech, for which I must
efer the Reader to Shakespear's Plays, & the
Prince made a still longer. Things being thus
ettled between them the King died, & was
ucceeded by his son Henry who had previously
eat Sir William Gascoigne.

Henry the 5th

Henry the 5th

C.E. Austen pinx:

This Prince after he succeeded to the throne

grew quite reformed & amiable, forsaking all his dissipated Companions, & never thrashing Sir William again. During his reign, Lord Cobham was burnt alive, but I forget what for. His Majesty then turned his thoughts to France, where he went & fought the famous Battle of Agincourt. He afterwards married the King's daughter Catherine, a very agreable Woman by Shakespear's account. Inspite of all this however he died, and was succeeded by his son Henry.

Henry the 6th

Henry the 6th

C E Austen pinx

I cannot say much for this Monarch's Sense— Nor would I if I could, for he was a Lancastrian. I suppose you know all about the Wars between him & the Duke of York who was of the right side; if you do not, you had better read some other History, for I shall not be very diffuse in this, meaning by it only to vent my Spleen against, & shew my Hatred to all those people whose parties or principles do not suit with mine, & not to give information. This King married Margaret of Anjou, a Woman whose distresses & Misfortunes were so great, as almost to make me who hate her, pity her. It was in this reign that Joan of Arc lived & made such a row among the English. They should not have burnt her — but they did. There were several Battles between the Yorkists &

Lancastrians, in which the former (as they on
usually conquered. At length they were entire
overcome; The King was murdered — The
Queen was sent home — & Edward the 4th
Ascended the Throne.

Edward the 4th

This Monarch was famous only for his Beauty & his Courage, of which the Picture we have here given of him, & his undaunted Behaviour in marrying one Woman while he was engaged to another, are sufficient knows. His Wife was Elizabeth Woodville, a Widow who, poor Woman! was afterwards confined in a Convent by that Monster of Iniquity & Avarice Henry the 7th. One of Edward's Mistresses was Jane Shore, who has had a play written about her, but it is a tragedy & therefore not worth reading. Having performed all these noble actions, his Majesty died, & was succeeded by his son.

Edward the 5th

This unfortunate Prince lived so little a while that nobody had time to draw his picture. He was murdered by his Uncle's Contrivance, whose name was Richard the 3d.

Richard the 3d

Rich the 3d

C E Austen pinx

The Character of this Prince has been in general very severely treated by Historians, but as he was a York, I am rather inclined to suppose him a very respectable Man. It has indeed been confidently asserted that he killed his two Nephews & his Wife, but it has also been declared that he did not kill his two Nephews, which I am inclined to believe true; & if this is the case, it may also be affirmed that he did not kill his Wife, for if Perkin Warbeck was really the Duke of York, why might not Lambert must be the widow of Richard. Whether innocent or guilty, she did not reign long in peace, for Henry Tudor E. of Richmond as great a villain as ever lived, made a great fuss about getting the Crown & having killed the King at the battle of Bosworth, he succeeded to it.

Henry the 7th

Henry the 7th

C Austen pinx:

This Monarch soon after his accession married the Princess Elizabeth of York, by which alliance he plainly proved that he thought his own right inferior to hers, tho' he pretended to the contrary. By this

Marriage he had two sons & two daughters, th
elder of which Daughters was married to the K.
of Scotland & had the happiness of being gran
-mother to one of the first Characters in the
World. But of her, I shall have occasion to spe
more at large in future. The Youngest, Mary
married first the King of France & secondly the
D. of Suffolk, by whom she had one daughte
afterwards the Mother of Lady Jane Grey,
who tho' inferior to her lovely Cousin the
Queen of Scots, was yet an amiable young
Woman & famous for reading Greek while
other people were hunting. It was in the
reign of Henry the 7th that Perkin Warbe
& Lambert Simnel before mentioned mad
their appearance, the former of whom which was
set in the Stocks, took shelter in Beaulie
Abbey, & was beheaded with the Earl of

Warwick, & the latter was taken into the Kings Kitchen. His Majesty died & was suc:ceeded by his son Henry whose only merit was his not being quite so bad as his ~~[illegible]~~ daughter Elizabeth.

Henry the 8th

~~It would be an~~

It would be an affront to my Readers were I to suppose that they were not as well acquainted with the particulars of this King's reign as I am myself. It will therefore be saving them the task of reading again what they have read before, & myself the trouble of writing what I do not perfectly recollect, by giving only a slight sketch of th principal Events which marked his reign Among these may be ranked Cardinal W -sey's telling the father Abbott of Leicester Abbey that "he was come to lay his bone among them," the reformation in Religio & the King's riding through the streets of London with Anna Bullen. It is however bu Justice, & my Duty to declare that this ami -able Woman was entirely innocent of the Crimes with which she was accused, of which he Beauty, her Elegance, & her Sprightliness w sufficient proofs, not to mention her solem protestations of Innocence, the weakness of the Charges against her, & the King's Charac -ter;

all of which add some confirmation, tho' perhaps
but slight ones when in comparison with
those before alledged in her favour. Tho' I do not
profess giving many dates, yet as I think
it proper to give some & shall of course
make choice of those which it is most necessary for the Reader to know, I think it
right to inform him that her letter to
the King was dated on the 6th of May.
The Crimes & Cruelties of this Prince, were
too numerous to be mentioned, (as this history I trust has fully shewn;) & nothing
can be said in his vindication, but that
his abolishing Religious Houses & leaving
them to the ruinous depredations of time
has been of infinite use to the landscape

of England in general, which probably was a principal motive for his doing it, since otherwise why should a Man who was of no Religion himself be at so much trouble to abolish one which had for ages been established in the Kingdom. His Majesty's 5th wife was the Duke of Norfolk's Neice who, tho' universally acquitted of the crimes for which she was beheaded, has been by many people supposed to have led an abandoned life before her Marriage— Of this however I have many doubts, since she was a relation of that noble Duke of Norfolk who was so warm in the Queen of Scotland's cause, & who at last fell a victim to it. The King's last wife contrived to survive him, but with difficulty effected it. He was succeeded by his only son Edward.

Edward the 6th

As this prince was only nine years old at the time of his Father's death, he was considered by many people as too young to govern, & the late King happening to be of the same opinion, his mother's Brother the Duke of Somerset was chosen Protector of the realm during his minority. This Man was on the whole of a very amiable Character, & is somewhat of a favourite with me, tho' I would by no means pretend to affirm that he was equal to those first of Men Robert Earl of Essex, Delamere, or Gilpin. He was beheaded, of which he might with reason have been proud, had he known that such was the death of Mary Queen of Scotland; but as it was impossible that he should be conscious of what had never happened, it does not appear that he felt particularly delighted with the manner of ~~[illegible]~~ it. After his decease the Duke of Northumberland had the care of the King & the Kingdom, & performed his trust of both so well that the King died & the Kingdom was left to his daughter in law

he Lady Jane Grey, who has been already mentioned as reading Greek. Whether she really understood that language or whether such a study
roceeded only from an excess of ~~Coxcombry~~ vanity
r which I believe she was always rather
markable, is uncertain. Whatever might
the cause, she preserved the same ap-
earance of knowledge, & contempt of what
s generally esteemed pleasure, during the
hole of her Life, for she declared herself
ispleased with being appointed Queen, and
hile conducting to the Scaffold, she wrote
sentence in latin & another in Greek
seeing the dead Body of her Husband
ccidentally passing that way.

Mary.

This woman had the good luck of being advanced to the throne of England, inspite of the superior pretensions, Merit, & Beauty of her Cousins Mary Queen of Scotland & Jane Grey. Nor can I pity the Kingdom for the misfortunes they experienced during her Reign, since they fully deserved them, for having allowed her to succeed her Brother which was a double piece of folly, since they might have foreseen that as she died without Children, she would be succeeded by that

disgrace to humanity, that pest of society, Eliza-
-beth. Many were the people who fell Martyrs
to the protestant Religion during her reign;
I suppose not fewer than a dozen. She mar-
-ried Philip King of Spain who in her Sister's
reign was famous for building Armadas. She died
without issue, & then the dreadful moment came
in which the destroyer of all comfort, the deceitful
Betrayer of trust reposed in her, & the Murderess of
her Cousin succeeded to the Throne. —

Elizabeth —

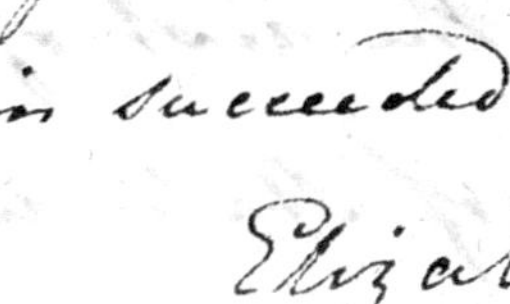

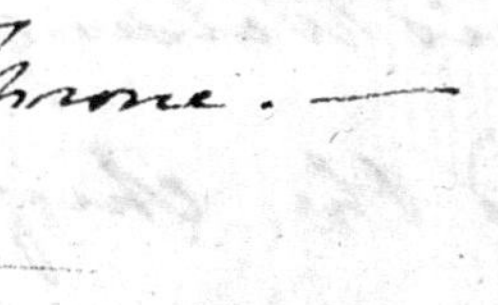

It was the peculiar misfortune of this Woman to have bad Ministers — Since wicked as she herself was, she could not have committed such extensive mis:=chief, had not these vile & abandoned Men connived at, & encouraged her in her Crimes. I know that it has by many people been asserted & beleived that Lord Burleigh, Sir Francis Walsingham, & the rest of those who filled the chief Offices of State were deserving, experienced, & able Ministers. But Oh! how blinded such Writers & such Readers must be to true Merit, to Merit despised, neglected & defamed, if they can persist in such opinions when they reflect that these Men, these boasted Men were

uch Scandals to their Country & their sex as to
llow & assist their Queen in confining for the
pace of nineteen Years, a <u>Woman</u> who if the
claims of Relationship & Merit were of no
vail, yet as a Queen & as one who condescended
place confidence in her, had every reason to
xpect Assistance & protection; and at length
allowing Elizabeth to bring this amiable
oman to an untimely, unmerited, and scandalous Death. Can any one if he reflects
ut for a moment on this blot, this everlasting blot upon their Understanding
their Character, allow any praise to Lord
urleigh or Sir Francis Walsingham? Oh! what
ust this bewitching Princess whose only
riend was then the Duke of Norfolk, and

whose only ones are now Mr Whitaker, Mrs Lefroy, Mrs Knight & myself, who was abandoned by her Son, confined by her Cousin, Abused, reproached & vilified by all, what must not her most noble Mind have suffered when informed that Elizabeth had given orders for her Death! Yet she bore it with a most unshaken fortitude; firm in her Mind; Constant in her Religion; & prepared herself to meet the cruel fate to which she was doomed, with a magnanimity that could alone proceed from conscious Innocence. And yet could you Reader have beleived it possible that some hardened & zealous Protestants have even abused her for that steadfastness in the Catholic Religion which reflected on her so much credit? But this is a striking proof of *their* narrow souls & prejudiced Judgements who accuse her. She was executed in the Great Hall at Fotheringay Castle (sacred Place!) on Wednesday the 8th of February - 1586 — to the everlasting Reproach of Elizabeth, her Ministers, and of England in general. It may not be unnecessary before I entirely conclude my account of this ill-fated Queen, to observe that she had been accused of several crimes during the time of her reigning in Scotland, of which I now most seriously do assure my Reader that she was entirely innocent; having never been guilty of anything more than Imprudencies into which she was betrayed by the openness of her Heart, her Youth, & her Education. Having I trust by this assurance entirely done away every Suspicion & every doubt which might have arisen in the Reader's mind, from what other Historians have written of her, I shall proceed to mention the remaining Events that marked Elizabeth's reign. It was about this time that Sir Francis Drake the first English Navigator who sailed round the World, lived, to be the ornament of his Country & his profession. Yet great as he was, & justly celebrated as a Sailor, I cannot help foreseeing that he will be equalled in this or the next Century by one who tho'

w
but young, already promises to answer all the ardent & sanguine expectations of his Relations & Friends, amongst whom I may class the amiable Lady to whom this work is dedicated, & my no less amiable Self.

Though of a different profession, and shining in a different Sphere of Life, yet equally conspicuous in the Character of an _Earl_, as Drake was in that of a _Sailor_, was Robert Devereux Lord Essex. This unfortunate young Man was not unlike in Character to that equally unfortunate one _Frederic Delamere_. The simile may be carried still farther, & Elizabeth the torment of Essex may be compared to the Emmeline of Delamere. It would be endless to recount the misfortunes of this noble & gallant Earl. It is sufficient to say that he was beheaded on the 25th of Feby, after having been Lord Leuitenant of Ireland, after having clapped his hand on his sword, and after performing many other services to his Country. Elizabeth did not long survive his loss, & died so miserable that were it not an injury to the memory of Mary I should pity her.

James the 1st

Though this King had some faults, among which & as the most principal, was his allowing his Mother's death, yet considered on the whole I cannot help liking him. He married Anne of Denmark, and had several Children; fortunately for him his eldest son Prince Henry died before his Father or he might have experienced the evils which befell his unfortunate Brother.

As I am myself partial to the roman catholic religion, it is with infinite regret that I am obliged to blame the Behaviour of any Member of it: yet Truth being I think very excusable in an Historian, I am necessitated to say that in this reign the roman Catholics of England did not behave like Gentlemen to the protestants. Their Behaviour indeed to the Royal Family & both Houses of Parliament might justly be considered by them as very uncivil, and even Sir Henry Percy tho' certainly the best bred Man of the party, had none of that general politeness which is so universally pleasing, as his Attentions were entirely confined to Lord Mounteagle.

Sir Walter Raleigh flourished in this & the preceding reign, & is by many people held in great veneration & respect — But as he was an enemy of the noble Essex, I have nothing to say in praise of him, & must refer all those who may wish to be acquainted with the particulars of his Life, to Mr Sheridan's play of the Critic, where they will find many interesting Anecdotes as well of him as of his friend Sir Christopher Hatton.—His Majesty was of that amiable disposition which inclines to Friendships, & in such points was possessed of a keener penetration in discovering Merit than many other people. I once heard an excellent Sharade on a Carpet, of which the subject I am now on reminds me, and as I think it may afford my Readers some Amusement to *find it out*, I shall here take the liberty of presenting it to them.

Sharade

My first is what my second was to King James the 1st, and you tread on my whole.

The principal favourites of his Majesty were Car, who was afterwards created Earl of Somerset and whose name perhaps may have some share in the above-mentioned Sharade & George Villiers afterwards Duke of Buckingham. On his Majesty's death he was succeeded by his son Charles.

Charles the 1st

This amiable Monarch seems born to have suffered Misfortunes equal to those of his

lovely Grandmother; misfortunes which he could
not deserve since he was her descendant.
Never certainly were there before so many
detestable Characters at one time in England
as in this period of its History; Never were
amiable Men so scarce. The number of
them throughout the whole Kingdom amount-
:ing only to five, besides the inhabitants
of Oxford who were always loyal to their
King & faithful to his interests. The names
of this noble five who never forgot the duty
of the subject, or swerved from their attach-
-ment to his Majesty, were as follows—

The King himself, ever stedfast in his
own support— Archbishop Laud, Earl of
Strafford, Viscount Faulkland & Duke of Ormond,

who were scarcely lefs strenuous or zealous in the cause. While the *Villains* of the time would make too long a list to be written or read; I shall therefore content myself with mentioning the leaders of the Gang. Cromwell, Fairfax, Hampden, & Pym may be considered as the original Causers of all the disturbances Distresses, & Civil Wars in which England for many years was embroiled. In this reign as well as in that of Elizabeth, I am obliged in spite of my attachment to the Scotch, to consider them as equally guilty with the generality of the English, since they dared to think differently from their Sovereign, to forget the Adoration which as

Subjects it was their Duty to pay them, to rebel against, dethrone & imprison the unfortunate Mary; to oppose, to deceive, and to sell the no less unfortunate Charles. The Events of this Monarch's reign are too numerous for my pen, and indeed the recital of any Events (except what I make myself) is ~~tedious~~ uninteresting to me; my principal reason for undertaking the History of England being to prove the innocence of the Queen of Scotland, which I flatter myself with having effectually done, and to abuse Elizabeth, tho' I am rather fearful of having fallen short in the latter part of my Scheme. — As therefore it is not

my intention to give any particular ac-
-count of the distresses into which this
King was involved through the miscon-
-duct & Cruelty of his Parliament, I
shall satisfy myself with vindicating
him from the Reproach of Arbitrary
& tyrannical Government with which
he has often been Charged. This, I feel,
is not difficult to be done, for with
one argument I am certain of satisfying
every sensible & well disposed person
whose opinions have been properly
guided by a good Education — & this
Argument is that he was a Stuart

Finis Saturday Nov: 26th 179

THE TRANSCRIPT

THE HISTORY OF ENGLAND

FROM THE REIGN OF

HENRY THE 4TH

TO THE DEATH OF

CHARLES THE 1ST

By a partial, prejudiced, & ignorant Historian

To Miss Austen, eldest daughter of the Revd. George Austen,

this Work is inscribed with all due respect by

The Author

N.B. There will be very few Dates in this History.

2 HENRY THE 4TH

Henry the 4th ascended the throne of England much to his own satisfaction in the year 1399, after having prevailed on his cousin & predecessor Richard the 2nd to resign it to him, & to retire for the rest of his Life to Pomfret Castle, where he happened to be murdered. It is to be supposed that Henry was married, since he had certainly four sons, but it is not in my
3 power to inform the Reader who was his wife. Be this as it may, he did / not live for ever, but falling ill, his son the Prince of Wales came and took away the crown; whereupon the King made a long speech, for which I must refer the Reader to Shakespear's Plays, & the Prince made a still longer. Things being thus settled between them the King died, & was succeeded by his son Henry who had previously beat Sir William Gascoigne.

HENRY THE 5TH

This Prince after he succeeded to the throne /
4 grew quite reformed and amiable, forsaking all his dissipated Companions, & never thrashing Sir William again. During his reign, Lord Cobham was burnt alive, but I forget what for. His Majesty then turned his thoughts to France, where he went & fought the famous Battle of Agincourt. He afterwards married the King's daughter Catherine, a very agreable Woman by Shakespear's account. Inspite of all this however, he died, and was succeeded by his son Henry.

HENRY THE 6TH /

I cannot say much for this Monarch's 5
sense. Nor would I if I could, for he was a Lancastrian. I suppose you know all about
the Wars between him & the Duke of York who was of the right side; if you do not,
you had better read some other History, for I shall not be very diffuse in this, meaning by it only to vent my Spleen *against*, & shew my Hatred *to* all those people
whose parties or principles do not suit with mine, & not to give information. This
King married Margaret of Anjou, a woman whose distresses & misfortunes were so
great as almost to make me who hate her, pity her. It was in this reign that Joan of
Arc lived & made such a *row* among the English. They should not have burnt
her—but they did. There were several Battles between the Yorkists & /
Lancastrians, in which the former (as they ought) usually conquered. At length 6
they were entirely overcome; The King was murdered—The Queen was sent
home—& Edward the 4th ascended the Throne.

EDWARD THE 4TH

This Monarch was famous only for his
Beauty & his Courage, of which the Picture we have here given of him, & his
undaunted Behaviour in marrying one Woman while he was engaged to another,
are sufficient / proofs. His Wife was Elizabeth Woodville, a Widow who, poor 7
Woman! was afterwards confined in a Convent by that Monster of Iniquity &
Avarice Henry the 7th. One of Edward's Mistresses was Jane Shore, who has had a
play written about her, but it is a tragedy & therefore not worth reading. Having
performed all these noble actions, his Majesty died, & was succeeded by his son.

EDWARD THE 5TH

This unfortunate Prince lived so little a while that nobody had time to draw his picture. He was murdered by his Uncle's Contrivance, whose name was Richard the 3rd. /

8 ## RICHARD THE 3RD

The Character of this Prince has been in general very severely treated by Historians, but as he was a *York*, I am rather inclined to suppose him a very respectable Man. It has indeed been confidently asserted that he killed his two Nephews & his Wife, but it has also been declared that he did *not* kill his two Nephews, which I am inclined to beleive true; & if this is the case, it may also be affirmed that he did not kill his Wife, for if Perkin Warbeck was really
9 the Duke of York, why might not Lambert / Simnel be the Widow of Richard.
Whether innocent or guilty, he did not reign long in peace, for Henry Tudor E. of Richmond as great a villain as ever lived, made a great fuss about getting the Crown & having killed the King at the battle of Bosworth, he succeeded to it.

HENRY THE 7TH

This monarch soon after his accession married the Princess Elizabeth of York, by which alliance he plainly proved that he thought his own right inferior to hers, tho' he pretended to the contrary. By this /

Marriage he had two sons & two daughters, the elder of which Daughters was mar- 10
ried to the King of Scotland & had the happiness of being grandmother to one of
the first Characters in the World. But of *her*, I shall have occasion to speak more at
large in future. The Youngest, Mary, married first the King of France & secondly the
D. of Suffolk, by whom she had one daughter, afterwards the Mother of Lady Jane
Grey, who tho' inferior to her lovely Cousin the Queen of Scots, was yet an amiable
young woman & famous for reading Greek while other people were hunting. It was
in the reign of Henry the 7th that Perkin Warbeck & Lambert Simnel before mentioned made their appearance, the former of whom was set in the Stocks, took shelter in Beaulieu Abbey, & was beheaded with the Earl of / Warwick, & the latter was 11
taken into the King's kitchen. His Majesty died & was succeeded by his son Henry
whose only merit was his not being *quite* so bad as his daughter Elizabeth.

HENRY THE 8TH

It would be an affront to my Readers were I
to suppose that they were not as well acquainted with the particulars of this King's
reign as I am myself. It will therefore be saving *them* the task of reading again what
they have read before, & *myself* the / trouble of writing what I do not perfectly rec- 12
ollect, by giving only a slight sketch of the principal Events which marked his reign.
Among these may be ranked Cardinal Wolsey's telling the father Abbott of
Leicester Abbey that 'he was come to lay his bones among them,' the reformation
in Religion, & the King's riding through the streets of London with Anna Bullen. It
is however but Justice, & my Duty to declare that this amiable Woman was entirely
innocent of the Crimes with which she was accused, of which her Beauty, her
Elegance, & her Sprightliness were sufficient proofs, not to mention her solemn
protestations of Innocence, the weakness of the Charges against her, & the King's
Character; / all of which add some confirmation, tho' perhaps but slight ones when 13

in comparison with those before alledged in her favour. Tho' I do not profess giving
many dates, yet as I think it proper to give some & shall of course make choice of
those which it is most necessary for the Reader to know, I think it right to inform
him that her letter to the King was dated on the 6th of May. The Crimes &
Cruelties of this Prince, were too numerous to be mentioned, (as this history I trust
has fully shewn) & nothing can be said in his vindication, but that his abolishing
Religious Houses & leaving them to the ruinous depredations of time has been of
14 infinite use to the landscape / of England in general, which probably was a principal
motive for his doing it, since otherwise why should a Man who was of no Religion
himself be at so much trouble to abolish one which had for ages been established in
the Kingdom. His Majesty's 5th wife was the Duke of Norfolk's Neice who, tho'
universally acquitted of the crimes for which she was beheaded, has been by many
people supposed to have led an abandoned Life before her Marriage—of this however I have many doubts, since she was a relation of that noble Duke of Norfolk
who was so warm in the Queen of Scotland's cause, & who at last fell a victim to it.
15 The Kings last / wife contrived to survive him, but with difficulty effected it. He
was succeeded by his only son Edward.

EDWARD THE 6TH

As this prince was only nine years old at
the time of his Father's death, he was considered by many people as too young to
govern, & the late King happening to be of the same opinion, his mother's Brother
16 the Duke of Somerset was chosen Protector of the realm during / his minority. This
Man was on the whole of a very amiable Character, & is somewhat of a favourite
with me, tho' I would by no means pretend to affirm that he was equal to those first

of Men Robert Earl of Essex, Delamare, or Gilpin. He was beheaded, of which he might with reason have been proud, had he known that such was the death of Mary Queen of Scotland; but as it was impossible that he should be conscious of what had never happened, it does not appear that he felt particularly delighted with the manner of it. After his decease the Duke of Northumberland had the care of the King & the Kingdom, & performed his trust of both so well that the King died & the
Kingdom was left to his daughter in law / the Lady Jane Grey, who has been already 17
mentioned as reading Greek. Whether she really understood that language or whether such a study proceeded only from an excess of vanity for which I beleive she was always rather remarkable, is uncertain. Whatever might be the cause, she preserved the same appearance of knowledge, & contempt of what was generally esteemed pleasure, during the whole of her Life, for she declared herself displeased with being appointed Queen, and while conducting to the Scaffold, she wrote a Sentence in Latin & another in Greek on seeing the dead Body of her husband accidentally passing that way. /

MARY 18

This woman had the good luck of being advanced to the throne of England, inspite of the superior pretensions, Merit, & Beauty of her Cousins Mary Queen of Scotland & Jane Grey. Nor can I pity the Kingdom for the misfortunes they experienced during her Reign, since they fully deserved them, for having allowed her to succeed her Brother—which was a double peice of folly, since they might have foreseen that as she died without Children, she
would be succeeded by that / disgrace to humanity, that pest of society, Elizabeth. 19
Many were the people who fell Martyrs to the protestant Religion during her reign;

I suppose not fewer than a dozen. She married Philip King of Spain who in her Sister's reign for famous for building Armadas. She died without issue, & then the dreadful moment came in which the destroyer of all comfort, the deceitful Betrayer of trust reposed in her, & the Murderess of her Cousin succeeded to the Throne.

ELIZABETH /

20 It was the peculiar Misfortune of this Woman to have had bad Ministers—Since wicked as she herself was, she could not have committed such extensive Mischeif, had not these vile & abandoned Men connived at, & encouraged her in her Crimes. I know that it has by many people been asserted & beleived that Lord Burleigh, Sir Francis Walsingham, & the rest of those who filled the chief Offices of State were deserving, experienced, & able Ministers. But oh! how blinded such Writers & such Readers must be to true Merit, to Merit despised, neglected & defamed, if they can persist in such opinions when
21 they reflect that these Men, these boasted Men were / such Scandals to their Country & their Sex as to allow & assist their Queen in confining for the space of nineteen years, a *Woman* who if the claims of Relationship & Merit were of no avail, yet as a Queen & as one who condescended to place confidence in her, had every reason to expect assistance & protection; and at length in allowing Elizabeth to bring this amiable Woman to an untimely, unmerited, and scandalous Death. Can any one if he reflects but for a moment on this blot, this everlasting blot upon their Understanding & their Character, allow any praise to Lord Burleigh or Sir Francis Walsingham? Oh! what must this bewitching Princess whose only freind
22 was then the Duke of Norfolk, and / whose only ones now Mr Whitaker, Mrs Lefroy, Mrs Knight & myself, who was abandoned by her son, confined by her

Cousin, abused, reproached & vilified by all, what must not her most noble mind
have suffered when informed that Elizabeth had given orders for her Death! Yet she
bore it with a most unshaken fortitude, firm in her Mind; Constant in her Religion;
& prepared herself to meet the cruel fate to which she was doomed, with a magnanimity that could alone proceed from conscious Innocence. And yet could you
Reader have beleived it possible that some hardened & zealous Protestants have
even abused her for that / steadfastness in the Catholic Religion which reflected on 23
her so much credit? But this is a striking proof of *their* narrow souls & prejudiced
Judgements who accuse her. She was executed in the Great Hall at Fotheringay
Castle (sacred Place!) on Wednesday the 8th of February—1585—to the everlasting Reproach of Elizabeth, her Ministers, and of England in general. It may not be
unnecessary before I entirely conclude my account of this ill-fated Queen, to
observe that she had been accused of several crimes during the time of her reigning
in Scotland, of which I now most seriously do assure my Reader that she was entirely innocent; having never been guilty of anything more / than Imprudencies into 24
which she was betrayed by the openness of her Heart, her Youth, & her Education.
Having I trust by this assurance entirely done away every Suspicion & every doubt
which might have arisen in the Reader's mind, from what other Historians have
written of her, I shall proceed to mention the remaining Events that marked
Elizabeth's reign. It was about this time that Sir Francis Drake the first English
Navigator who sailed round the World, lived, to be the ornament of his Country &
his profession. Yet great as he was, & justly celebrated as a Sailor, I cannot help
foreseeing that he will be equalled in this or the next Century by one who tho' /
now but young, already promises to answer all the ardent & sanguine expectations 25
of his Relations & Freinds, amongst whom I may class the amiable Lady to whom
this work is dedicated, & my no less amiable Self.

Though of a different profession, and shining in a different Sphere of Life, yet equally conspicuous in the Character of an *Earl*, as Drake was in that of a *Sailor*,

was Robert Devereux Lord Essex. This unfortunate young Man was not unlike in Character to that equally unfortunate one *Frederic Delamere*. The simile may be carried still farther, & Elizabeth the torment of Essex may be compared to the
26 Emmeline of Delamere. It would be endless / to recount the misfortunes of this
noble & gallant Earl. It is sufficient to say that he was beheaded on the 25th of Feb:ry, after having been Lord Leuitenant of Ireland, after having clapped his hand on his sword, and after performing many other services to his Country. Elizabeth did not long survive his loss, & died *so* miserable that were it not an injury to the memory of Mary I should pity her.

JAMES THE 1ST /

27 Though this King had some faults, among
which & as the most principal, was his allowing his Mother's death, yet considered on the whole I cannot help liking him. He married Anne of Denmark, and had several Children; fortunately for him his eldest son Prince Henry died before his father or he might have experienced the evils which befell his unfortunate Brother.

As I am myself partial to the roman catholic religion, it is with infinite regret that I am obliged to blame the Behaviour of any Member of it: yet Truth being I think very excusable in an Historian, I am necessitated to say that in this reign
28 the roman Catholics of England did not / behave like Gentlemen to the protes-
tants. Their Behaviour indeed to the Royal Family & both Houses of Parliament might justly be considered by them as very uncivil, and even Sir Henry Percy tho' certainly the best bred Man of the party, had none of that general politeness which is so universally pleasing, as his attentions were entirely confined to Lord Mounteagle.

Sir Walter Raleigh flourished in this & the preceding reign, & is by many people held in great veneration & respect—But as he was an enemy of the noble Essex, I have nothing to say in praise of him, & must refer all those who may wish
to be acquainted with the particulars of his Life, / to Mr Sheridan's play of the 29
Critic, where they will find many interesting Anecdotes as well of him as of his freind Sir Christopher Hatton.—His Majesty was of that amiable disposition which inclines to Freindship, & in such points was possessed of a keener penetration in Discovering Merit than many other people. I once heard an excellent Sharade on a Carpet, of which the subject I am now on reminds me, and as I think it may afford my Readers some amusement to *find it out*, I shall here take the liberty of presenting it to them.

Sharade

My first is what my second was to King James the 1st, and you tread on my whole. /

The principal favourites of his Majesty were Car, who was afterwards created 30
Earl of Somerset and whose name perhaps may have some share in the abovementioned Sharade, & George Villiers afterwards Duke of Buckingham. On his Majesty's death he was succeeded by his son Charles.

CHARLES THE 1ST

This amiable Monarch seems born to have
suffered Misfortunes equal to those of his / lovely Grandmother; Misfortunes which 31
he could not deserve since he was her descendant. Never certainly were there before so many detestable Characters at one time in England as in this period of its History; never were amiable Men so scarce. The number of them throughout the

whole Kingdom amounting only to *five*, besides the inhabitants of Oxford who were
always loyal to their King & faithful to his interests. The names of this noble five
who never forgot the duty of the Subject, or swerved from their attachment to his
Majesty, were as follows—The King himself, ever stedfast in his own support—
32 Archbishop Laud, Earl of Strafford, Viscount Faulkland & Duke of Ormond, / who
were scarcely less strenuous or zealous in the cause. While the *Villains* of the time
would make too long a list to be written or read; I shall therefore content myself
with mentioning the leaders of the Gang. Cromwell, Fairfax, Hampden, & Pym
may be considered as the original Causers of all the disturbances, Distresses, & Civil
Wars in which England for many years was embroiled. In this reign as well as in
that of Elizabeth, I am obliged in spite of my attachment to the Scotch, to consider
them as equally guilty with the generality of the English, since they dared to think
33 differently from their Sovereign, to forget the Adoration which as / *Stuarts* it was
their Duty to pay them, to rebel against, dethrone & imprison the unfortunate
Mary; to oppose, to deceive, and to sell the no less unfortunate Charles. The Events
of this Monarch's reign are too numerous for my pen, and indeed the recital of any
Events (except what I make myself) is uninteresting to me; my principal reason for
undertaking the History of England being to prove the innocence of the Queen of
Scotland, which I flatter myself with having effectually done, and to abuse
Elizabeth, tho' I am rather fearful of having fallen short in the latter part of my
34 Scheme.—.As therefore it is not / my intention to give any particular account of
the distresses into which this King was involved through the misconduct & Cruelty
of his Parliament, I shall satisfy myself with vindicating him from the Reproach of
arbitrary & tyrannical Government with which he has often been charged. This, I
feel, is not difficult to be done, for with one argument I am certain of satisfying
every sensible & well disposed person whose opinions have been properly guided by
a good Education—& this Argument is that he was a STUART.

Finis *Saturday Nov: 26th 1791*